Learn With Animals

On the Savanna

By Laura Ottina
Adapted by Barbara Bakowski

Illustrated by
Sebastiano Ranchetti

WEEKLY READER®
PUBLISHING

2

We live on the savanna,
And roam the grassy plain.
Winter here is long and dry,
But summertime brings rain.

I am a giraffe.
I eat leaves from tall trees.
I stretch my long neck
To reach them with ease.

5

6

I am a white rhino
With two horns that are large.
When I am angry,
At full speed I charge!

I am a male lion.
Of my yellow mane I'm proud.
I prowl the savanna,
Roaring deep and loud.

9

10

I am a gazelle
With big ears to help me hear.
I swiftly run from danger
When an enemy is near.

I am a zebra
With stripes of black and white.
My strong front teeth
Have a powerful bite!

13

14

I am an ostrich,
A bird too big to fly,
So I run on the ground
Instead of taking to the sky.

I am a hippo
With nostrils on my snout.
I can breathe underwater
Because my nose sticks out!

17

I am an elephant,
The biggest beast on land.
I have a pair of floppy ears
And ivory tusks so grand.

I am a baboon
With a pouch in my cheek
That I fill with the fruits,
Seeds, and berries I seek.

21

I am a vulture.
I soar high in the skies.
Then I swoop down for food
That I see with my sharp eyes.

Please visit our web site at **www.garethstevens.com**.
For a free catalog describing our list of high-quality books,
call 1-800-542-2595 (USA) or 1-800-387-3178 (Canada).
Our fax: 1-877-542-2596

Library of Congress Cataloging-in-Publication Data

Ottina, Laura.
   [Incontra gli animali nella savana. English]
   On the savanna / by Laura Ottina ; adapted by Barbara Bakowski ;
illustrated by Sebastiano Ranchetti.
      p. cm. — (Learn with animals)
   ISBN-10: 1-4339-1916-8   ISBN-13: 978-1-4339-1916-9 (lib. bdg.)
   ISBN-10: 1-4339-2093-X   ISBN-13: 978-1-4339-2093-6 (softcover)
   1. Savanna animals–Juvenile literature.   I. Bakowski, Barbara.
II. Ranchetti, Sebastiano, ill. III. Title.
QL115.308813   2010
591.7'48-dc22   2008052452

This North American edition first published in 2010 by
Weekly Reader® Books
An Imprint of Gareth Stevens Publishing
1 Reader's Digest Road
Pleasantville, NY 10570-7000 USA

Gareth Stevens Executive Managing Editor: Lisa M. Herrington
Gareth Stevens Senior Editor: Barbara Bakowski
Gareth Stevens Creative Director: Lisa Donovan
Gareth Stevens Designer: Jennifer Ryder-Talbot

Printed in the United States of America

1 2 3 4 5 6 7 8 9 12 11 10 09

Find out more about Laura Ottina and Sebastiano Ranchetti at **www.animalsincolor.com**.